Fossil Ridge Public Library District
386 Kennedy Road
Braidwood, Illinois 60408

4/02

High Blood Pressure

by Susan R. Gregson

Consultant:
Bijoy K. Khandheria, MD, FACC
Professor of Medicine, Mayo Medical School
Consultant, Cardiovascular Diseases and Internal Medicine
Mayo Clinic
Rochester, Minnesota

Perspectives on Disease and Illness

Fossil Ridge Public Library District
Braidwood, IL 60408

LifeMatters
an imprint of Capstone Press
Mankato, Minnesota

LifeMatters books are published by Capstone Press
PO Box 669 • 151 Good Counsel Drive • Mankato, Minnesota 56002
http://www.capstone-press.com

Printed in the United States of America

Library of Congress Cataloging-in-Publication Data
Gregson, Susan R.
      High blood pressure / by Susan R. Gregson.
          p.   cm. — (Perspectives on disease and illness)
      Includes bibliographical references and index.
      ISBN 0-7368-0750-0
      1. Hypertension—Juvenile literature. [1. Hypertension. 2. Circulatory system.] I. Title. II. Series.
      RC685.H8 G69 2001
      616.1´32—dc21   00-010423
                                                  CIP

Summary: Defines hypertension and why teens should care about it. Explores the role of the circulatory system, as well as some causes and risks of high blood pressure. Discusses diagnosis and treatment and how teens can lead a heart-healthy lifestyle.

Staff Credits
Charles Pederson, editor; Adam Lazar, designer; Kim Danger, photo researcher
Cover production by Anne Schafer
Interior production by Stacey Field

Photo Credits
Cover: ©DigitalVision, left; ©Artville/Clair Alaska, middle; ©DigitalVision/Ronnie Eshel, right; Stock Market/©Howard Sochurek, bottom
©Artville/Clair Alaska, 25; Don Carstens, 37
©DigitalVision, 7, 17, 35
International Stock/©Charlie Westerman, 21; ©Tony Demin, 44; ©Johnny Stockshooter, 50
©PhotoDisc/Barbara Penoyar, 57; 59
Photri Inc./©Fotopic, 43
Unicorn Stock Photos/©Tom McCarthy, 32; ©Martin R. Jones, 55
Uniphoto Picture Agency, 45/©Les Moore, 10; ©Mark W. Lisk, 26

Table of Contents

Chapter Overview

High blood pressure (HBP) is more than a rise in blood pressure. It is a dangerous condition.

Blood pressure is described as one number "over" another.

Anyone can have high blood pressure. Many people don't even realize they have it.

Low blood pressure also isn't good.

You can act now to prevent getting HBP later. This includes eating right, not smoking, and exercising regularly.

Chapter 1

What Is High Blood Pressure?

Have you ever felt so angry that your skin got hot and your face got red? Maybe you've had a friend tell you to "chill out," "take a chill pill," or "get a grip." You even may have said, "I'm so angry, my blood pressure must be through the roof."

Many of us think of times like these as when our blood pressure rises. For some people, blood pressure does rise a little when they're scared, angry, excited, or upset. Feeling stress can raise your blood pressure. But high blood pressure (HBP), or hypertension, is more than just a brief rise in the pressure. It means that your blood pressure is high over a long period of time.

High blood pressure is mentioned in China as early as 2000 B.C. The Chinese called it "the hard pulse."

Blood pressure is the force of your blood on your artery walls. You need blood pressure so your blood can travel from your heart to your organs and muscles. Your body needs the nutrients and oxygen from your blood. Nutrients are substances your body needs to stay healthy. If you didn't have any blood pressure, your heart wouldn't be beating.

High blood pressure is dangerous. When blood pressure stays too high for too long, it can damage your blood vessels. Organs such as your kidneys, heart, brain, and eyes can be affected. HBP makes your heart work harder to pump. This may make it become larger or begin to fail.

High blood pressure is the leading risk factor for heart failure. HBP also increases your risk later for atherosclerosis, or hardening of the arteries. Over time, atherosclerosis hardens, scars, and thickens your arteries. Some of these changes in your arteries might happen as you grow older, but HBP makes them happen sooner.

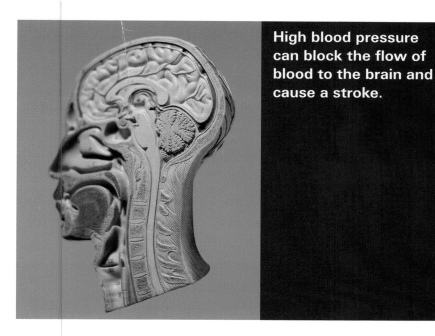

High blood pressure can block the flow of blood to the brain and cause a stroke.

Sometimes, high blood pressure can cause a stroke. This happens when a blood vessel carrying blood to the brain is blocked or breaks. No blood reaches the brain, and neither does the oxygen in the blood. It's the lack of oxygen that causes the stroke. A stroke can affect your movement, speech, and vision, or even kill you.

Strokes are not just for older people. Nearly 30 percent of all strokes happen in people younger than age 65. Often, high blood pressure has no symptoms or signs until a stroke happens. That's why some people call HBP a silent killer.

Toni's doctor told her that she has hypertension. "I have *what?*" Toni asked.

Toni, Age 18

Toni's dad told the doctor that Toni was the calmest person he knew. "My daughter never gets upset and is so easygoing," he said. Dr. Sholtis explained that hypertension doesn't mean you're hyper or tense. It means that your blood pressure is higher than normal. Too much pressure is in your arteries from your pumping blood.

Did You Know?

Salt and sodium aren't the same thing. Salt is made up of sodium and chloride. However, many people use the word *salt* when they mean *sodium*.

What the Numbers Mean

Every time your heart beats, it pumps blood around your body. Pressure is needed for blood to reach all parts of the body. Two numbers are used to describe blood pressure. Your health care professional will say that your blood pressure is one number "over" another number. For example, Toni's blood pressure was 148 over 92 the last three times it was measured. The nurse read the number as "148 over 92." You may see it written with a slash: 148/92.

The first number records the systolic pressure. That's the pressure inside your arteries when your heart pumps. The second number records the diastolic pressure. That's the pressure in your arteries when your heart relaxes and refills with blood. The American Heart Association defines high blood pressure for an adult as a reading of 140 over 90 or higher. A normal range for adults over age 18 is less than 130 over 85. The best reading is less than 120 over 80, although low blood pressure can be a problem, too.

Blood pressure in children and teens can vary depending on age, height, weight, and other factors. So, a doctor must decide what's considered normal or high blood pressure for a child or teen. Chapter 4 will talk more about measuring blood pressure.

High Blood Pressure

Myth: You should stay away from hot tubs and saunas if you have high blood pressure.

Fact: People with high blood pressure who have no active symptoms should be able to use saunas and hot tubs. Blood vessels relax in a sauna about as much as they relax when you walk quickly. However, if you have chest pain or are short of breath, you should not use hot tubs or saunas. Also, moving back and forth between cold water baths and hot water can raise blood pressure. People with high blood pressure should not do this.

Who Gets High Blood Pressure?

Anyone can have high blood pressure. Nearly 50 million people in the United States alone have high blood pressure. That's about 20 percent of the population over the age of 6. Almost 3 million kids ages 6 to 17 have HBP. About one-fourth of Canadians have high blood pressure. Of all the people who have HBP, nearly one-third don't even know they have it.

Some people are at a higher risk than others to develop the condition. If other people in your family have high blood pressure, you're at a greater risk of having it. If you're African American or of nonwhite Hispanic background, you're more likely than other people to develop HBP. Family history or ethnic background are risk factors that you can't control. You can control many risk factors, though. If you're overweight, smoke, don't exercise, or eat too much sodium, your chances of having HBP increase. Chapter 3 talks more about these HBP risk factors.

Someone in your neighborhood probably has high blood pressure.

The Other Side of the Coin

Just as there is high blood pressure, there also is low blood pressure. The definition of low blood pressure varies and is different for men and women. One study defined low blood pressure as below 115 over 70 for men and below 105 over 65 for women.

In some countries, low blood pressure is considered a sign of good health. In others, doctors feel that low blood pressure is linked to feeling weak and tired. Other studies suggest that low blood pressure can be related to depression, shock, or other conditions. More people, by far, have high blood pressure than low blood pressure. HBP causes more serious problems than low blood pressure does.

Jump Start Your Blood Pressure Smarts

"I can't have high blood pressure," Toni said. "I'm too young."

Toni, Age 18

"You're not too young to have HBP," explained Dr. Sholtis. "And you're not too young to control it."

Most teens don't have high blood pressure. Many adults do, however. Someone in your family and neighborhood probably has HBP. Learning all you can about HBP can help you lower your own risk of getting it. When you understand HBP, you also can help your loved ones with HBP.

Reducing your risk of high blood pressure starts with the habits you develop as a child and teen. Both good and bad habits are hard to break. Starting healthy lifestyle habits now will help you fight high blood pressure in the future. More and more young people have high blood pressure and are overweight. It's likely that these teens will become unhealthy adults. If you already have HBP, you can help control it with lifestyle changes, too.

Your adult body will have about 1.5 gallons (5 to 6 liters) of blood moving around it.

You can do several important things to control or prevent high blood pressure. These include eating a low-fat, low-salt diet, not smoking, and exercising regularly. If you don't have HBP, things you learn to do now can help prevent HBP later. Getting a jump on HBP now can help you look and feel better and protect you in the future.

High blood pressure is the most common chronic adult condition in America. Preventing and controlling high blood pressure is a lifelong commitment.

At a Glance

Points to Consider

Why do you think low blood pressure might be bad?

If one of your parents has high blood pressure, what do you think that might mean for you?

Next time you go to the doctor, ask about your blood pressure reading. Is it high, normal, or low? How do you feel about that?

Chapter Overview

Blood is part of your body's cardiovascular system. *Cardiovascular* means of the heart and circulation.

Blood moves through your heart, lungs, and body to carry oxygen to your muscles and organs.

Everyone needs blood pressure to move blood around his or her body. Some people have high blood pressure, though. This makes their heart work harder.

High blood pressure increases your risk for heart problems and stroke. It can damage your eyes and kidneys, too.

Chapter 2

Circulation:
The Blood's Superhighway

Your blood is part of your body's cardiovascular system. The cardiovascular system is made up of your heart, blood, and blood vessels. *Cardiovascular* means the heart (cardio) and circulatory (vascular) system of your body. Your blood vessels include the arteries and veins that carry blood to and from your heart. The heart pumps blood that is full of oxygen and nutrients. Your arteries and veins move the blood around your body to tissues and organs. Your circulatory system also helps your body get rid of waste.

The hypothalamus, which is a part of your brain, regulates your body's blood pressure.

Veins and arteries also are called blood vessels. They're relatively large. Other blood vessels are called capillaries, venules, and smaller arterioles. Your heart moves blood through your blood vessels.

There are two groups of blood vessels in your cardiovascular system. These groups, or pathways, are called the pulmonary circuit and the systemic circuit. Pulmonary blood vessels carry blood back and forth between the lungs and heart. Systemic blood vessels carry blood between the heart and everywhere else in your body.

Ruby was getting her blood drawn for a test. "Hey," she said to the nurse, "why are the lines on my arm blue if the blood inside is red?" The nurse smiled and said, "Oxygen, Ruby."

Ruby, Age 12

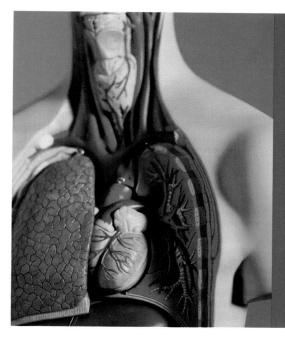

Your body has two groups of blood vessels. Some carry blood to the heart. Some carry it away from the heart.

How Blood Hitches a Ride in Your Body

Here's what Ruby's nurse meant. When you breathe, your lungs fill with air. Oxygen in the air passes through the air sacs in your lungs, where your blood picks it up. It's now oxygenated blood, or filled with oxygen. The oxygen gives blood its red color. The blood travels to the heart, which pumps it through the arteries to other parts of your body.

As the blood moves through the circulatory system, it releases oxygen into the tissues and organs. The blood picks up waste carbon dioxide as it releases oxygen. Instead of oxygen, the blood now carries carbon dioxide, which makes the blood look blue.

Veins carry the blood with carbon dioxide back to the heart. The heart pumps the blood back into your lungs, where the carbon dioxide is dropped off. You breathe out the carbon dioxide when you exhale. When you breathe in, your blood picks up more oxygen in your lungs. The ride starts all over on your body's circulation superhighway.

British physiologist Stephen Hales (1677–1761) was the first person to measure blood pressure in the arteries of mammals.

Lars and Fran, Age 15

Lars reached across the cafeteria table and grabbed Fran's potato chips. He tossed some carrot sticks on her tray. "Why are you messing with my lunch?" Fran said.

"Come on," said Lars. "My grandma has high blood pressure, and the doc told her to watch what she eats."

"I'm not your grandma," said Fran, making a face at Lars.

"But I want you around for a long time," said Lars. "And grandma's doc says you're never too young to start preventing HBP."

"It's a good thing I like carrots . . . and you," laughed Fran as she nibbled the carrot sticks.

High Blood Pressure

London doctor William Harvey (1578–1657) first wrote about how the heart works and how blood moves around the human body. People did not fully accept his ideas until the 1800s, when more studies proved his theories.

At a Glance

Why High Blood Pressure Is Bad

High blood pressure is bad. People with HBP are three times more likely than other people to get coronary heart disease, or clogged arteries. They are six times more likely to develop heart failure and seven times more likely to have a stroke.

If that's not enough to make you run for the no-salt pretzels, HBP makes your heart work harder. A little hard work in the form of exercise is good for your heart. But HBP makes your heart work hard all the time. Over time, this weakens the heart and arteries.

A heart that's only a little larger than normal might work okay. But a heart that always wrestles with high blood pressure can grow large and weak. You may become tired and weary. Your blood may not move all the way to your feet and hands, making them feel cold. This can lead to swelling of the ankles, feet, and sometimes the entire leg.

"My older sister had a stroke last year. The doctor said it was a minor one. She still limps a little, but you really can't tell she had a stroke otherwise. We were scared for her for a while, though. Because my sister had a stroke, my family knows the warning signs now. Call 9-1-1 if you have any of these signs or are with someone who has them:

• Numbness or weakness in the face, arm, or leg, especially on one side of the body

• Trouble speaking and understanding

• Trouble seeing

• Trouble walking, or feeling dizzy or off balance

• Painful headache with no reason"

—Gerald, age 17

Over time, your arteries will harden and scar. Hard, scarred arteries attract fatty deposits faster. Your arteries narrow and become clogged. A blood clot can form in one of your arteries and block blood flow. This can cause a stroke, heart attack, or even death.

Chronic high blood pressure can damage your eyes and kidneys, too. This can occur if the arteries that supply blood to these organs become hard. The blood flow is reduced or cut off, and the lack of oxygen can cause damage.

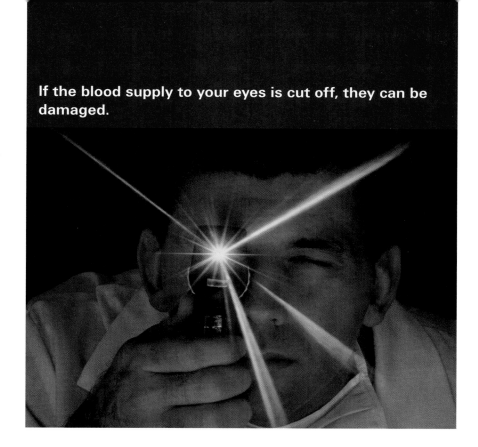

If the blood supply to your eyes is cut off, they can be damaged.

You can see how important it is to maintain good circulation in your body. Without it, the consequences may become serious.

Points to Consider

Place your fingers on the underside of your wrist or on the side of your neck. Can you feel the blood pulsing through your veins? What do you think of that?

Why do you think high blood pressure can make your heart weak?

If you don't have high blood pressure, should you worry about getting it later? Why or why not?

Chapter Overview

There are two kinds of high blood pressure: essential and secondary. Most people with HBP have essential hypertension. There is no known cause for essential hypertension.

You can prevent and control HBP by managing your risk factors. Some risk factors such as heredity and gender can't be changed. Others, such as being overweight or smoking, can be changed.

You can control other risk factors. These include how often you exercise, what you eat, and how you react to stress.

Chapter 3

Causes and Risks

Bad News and Good News

First the bad news. Doctors agree that 95 percent of the time, high blood pressure has no known cause. This means that a doctor usually can't find a specific thing that causes a person's blood pressure to stay high. HBP without a specific cause is called essential hypertension.

High blood pressure with a specific cause is called secondary hypertension. For example, kidney disease could cause HBP. Only 5 percent of high blood pressure is secondary hypertension.

You don't have to eat salt to spice up your meals. Try these simple ideas to add flavor to your food:

- Use a dash of salt-free Italian seasoning in your boiling water to cook pasta.

- Squeeze lemon juice onto your veggies, fish, or rice for a light, refreshing zing.

- Season your favorite potato salad with garlic-flavored vinegar instead of salt.

- Make your soup tastier with a few sprinkles of salt-free garlic and herb seasoning.

The good news is 95 percent of high blood pressure cases can be controlled, even HBP without a specific cause. This is done by changing the risk factors that can lead to HBP. The more risk factors you control now, the less likely you are to develop HBP. This is true even if your family has a history of it.

Risks You Can't Control

There are some risk factors for HBP that you can't control:

Your age. As you grow older, your blood pressure gradually rises. Most people over age 65 have blood pressure that could be considered above normal.

Your gender. Some studies show that men—especially younger men—might have a greater risk of HBP than women do. Women sometimes develop high blood pressure when they are pregnant. Doctors watch women who use birth-control pills to prevent pregnancy. Women who use the pill and who are overweight are more likely to develop high blood pressure. So are women who use the pill and have a family history of HBP or have mild kidney disease.

You can't control your age, gender, race, or family health history. However, you can control other risk factors.

Your family health history and race. If your parents have HBP, you're more likely to develop it. People of African descent have more blood pressure problems than people of other races do.

The body's reaction to salt. One researcher estimates that about 25 percent of people are extremely sensitive to salt. Even slight amounts of salt can raise their blood pressure.

What Can You Control?

Although you can't control some risk factors, you can control many factors to lower your risk of HBP. Much of this change means focusing on lifestyle habits. Sometimes, you may need to take medicine to control your risk factors. The next chapter talks more about medications. Chapter 5 discusses ways to change your lifestyle.

Choose to lose weight. Often, losing just a few pounds will lower your blood pressure. Losing weight has many other benefits. It reduces your risk of illnesses such as heart disease and diabetes. This is a disease in which too much sugar is in the blood.

Exercise is a good way to control high blood pressure.

Choose to move. If you don't exercise regularly, you will not be your healthiest. Regular exercise helps prevent obesity. Lack of activity greatly increases your chances of heart attack and stroke. Exercise!

Say no to cigarettes. Smoking isn't directly linked to high blood pressure, but it is a major risk factor for strokes.

Say yes to relaxation. Learn to manage stress, which can lead to smoking more and eating more. These are both bad habits if you want to prevent HBP. Relax for short periods during your school and workday. Do something you like on the weekends.

Never say diet. Eat balanced, low-fat, low-sodium, fruit-rich, and veggie-rich meals. Control the amount of cholesterol you eat, too. Cholesterol is a waxy, fatty substance your liver produces. There are two kinds of cholesterol. LDL is sometimes called bad cholesterol because it can clog your arteries. HDL is good cholesterol. It carries most of the bad cholesterol out of your blood.

High Blood Pressure

The U.S. Food and Drug Administration (FDA) has guidelines for labeling manufactured food products. Some of these guidelines deal with the amount of sodium in a food.

- *Sodium-free* means that there is less than 5 milligrams of sodium in each serving.

- *Very low-sodium* means the food has no more than 35 milligrams of sodium per serving.

- *Low-sodium* food has no more than 140 milligrams of sodium per serving.

- *Unsalted, no salt added,* or *without added salt* mean the food was prepared without adding more salt. Check the ingredients, though. Many foods still have salt or sodium as a natural part of the food itself.

Chapter 5 discusses some ways to eat healthy foods and add flavor to your meals. With a little preparation, you can have healthy snacks instead of fatty, salty junk food.

Mark looked at the paper on his desk in health class. It was a quiz about his risk factors for HBP. His teacher explained that the students wouldn't get a grade for this quiz. Mark read it and circled his answers. When he was done, he was shocked to discover he was "high blood pressure waiting to happen."

Mark, Age 14

The risk quiz Mark took in health class appears on the next page. You can try it, too. Chapter 5 provides more information about ways to turn bad blood pressure habits into good ones.

Quick Risk Quiz

On a separate piece of paper, write your answer for each question. The more times you answer "yes" or "don't know," the greater your risk of high blood pressure.

1. I smoke............................. Yes No Don't Know

2. I live with someone who smokes..... Yes No Don't Know

3. My total cholesterol is above 240..... Yes No Don't Know

4. My good cholesterol (HDL)
   is below 35......................... Yes No Don't Know

5. I don't know my cholesterol levels.... Yes No Don't Know

6. My blood pressure is 140 over 90
   or higher........................... Yes No Don't Know

7. I'm 20 pounds (9 kilograms) or more
   overweight.......................... Yes No Don't Know

8. I exercise less than a total of 30–45
   minutes at least three times a week... Yes No Don't Know

9. I have diabetes...................... Yes No Don't Know

High blood pressure causes about 50 percent of all strokes.

10. I take medicine to control my
    blood sugar.......................... Yes   No   Don't Know

11. I have a close male relative who
    had a heart attack before he was 55.... Yes   No   Don't Know

12. I have a close female relative who
    had a heart attack before she was 65... Yes   No   Don't Know

13. I have an abnormal or irregular
    heartbeat............................. Yes   No   Don't Know

14. I have coronary heart disease or have
    had a heart attack.................... Yes   No   Don't Know

Points to Consider

Can you think of one or two risk factors for high blood pressure that you might have? What do you think they are?

Name two things you can do right now to lower your risk of developing HBP.

The next time you're at the store, look for one kind of food that has a lot of sodium in it. Did you expect it to have a lot? Why or why not?

Chapter Overview

Having high blood pressure doesn't mean you're sick. However, you need to control HBP to keep from getting sick.

Blood pressure is measured with a sphygmomanometer.

Your doctor will take a number of readings to make sure you have HBP. The doctor also will ask questions about your medical history, check you physically, and conduct some tests.

You can control HBP with lifestyle changes, medication, or both.

Chapter 4

Diagnosing and Treating HBP

Having high blood pressure doesn't necessarily mean that you're sick. It does mean that you have a condition that can make you sick if you don't manage it. Untreated HBP means more risk for heart attack, stroke, and damage to certain organs. So the first step to managing HBP is diagnosing it, or figuring out if a person has it. This is true especially because there are usually no symptoms. Fortunately, measuring your blood pressure is quick, easy, and painless.

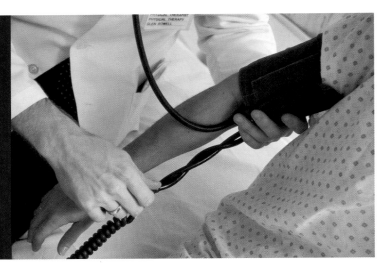

A sphygmomanometer is an instrument that measures blood pressure.

A "Sfig"-What?

A sphygmomanometer is used to measure blood pressure. That's a mouthful, but it's just the rubber cuff you've probably seen in a clinic or hospital. A nurse or doctor wraps the cuff around your arm and squeezes a bulb until the cuff inflates. The person reading your pressure places a stethoscope on your skin at the bend of your elbow. A stethoscope is used to listen to your heart and lungs. The inflated cuff stops blood flow in a large artery in your arm for just a moment.

The person reading your blood pressure listens to the stethoscope for sounds in your artery. At the same time, the person watches a gauge that looks like a large thermometer. It measures your blood pressure in millimeters of mercury. You can watch the silver liquid go up and down the gauge as the cuff is inflated and deflated.

The person who listens to the blood in your arm and watches the gauge is recording two measurements. The pressure reading on the gauge when the first sound is heard is the systolic pressure. This is the pressure when your heart beats. The diastolic measure is recorded when the last sound between heartbeats is heard. The measurement is recorded as one number "over" another, such as 120 over 80.

Sometimes pain, stress, or nervousness can make blood pressure rise temporarily. Normally, the reading is taken three to five minutes after the cuff is placed on the arm. This is to be sure that your anxiety isn't causing your reading to be higher than it should be.

Your doctor will not diagnose HBP if you have only one reading out of the normal range. Remember that for adults, a normal reading is below 130 over 85. If your reading is above 140 over 90, your doctor will have you return for another reading. It takes two or more high readings before HBP is diagnosed. This chart shows the ranges for high blood pressure.

Range	Type of high blood pressure
140/90 to 150/99	Mild
160/100 to 179/109	Moderate
180/110 to 209/119	Severe
210/120 or higher	Very severe

May's doctor told her on her third visit **May, Age 16** that she probably had high blood pressure. Her last three blood pressure readings were all above 140 over 90. Each time May visited the doctor to have her blood pressure measured, the doctor asked her questions and poked and prodded her. May felt like a trapped rat. When she told her doctor how she felt, the doctor explained what he was doing. He also told her why it was important for May to know about her HBP. He gave May materials to take home and read.

What to Expect When the Pressure Keeps Rising

May's doctor did a number of things to see if she had high blood pressure. Your doctor might do some of the same things for you. These usually include:

Taking blood pressure measurements repeatedly. These repeated measurements are needed to make sure that your blood pressure is consistently high. Instead of taking several short measurements, your doctor may monitor your blood pressure for six hours.

Asking about medical and family history. When your family members have high blood pressure, you are likely to have it, too.

High Blood Pressure

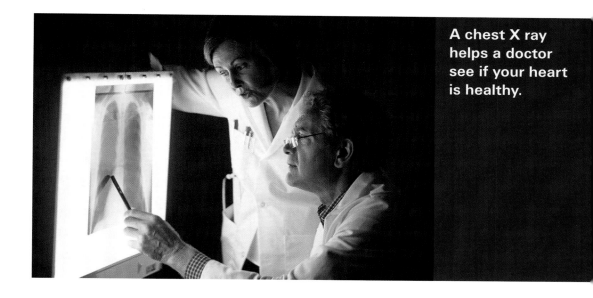

A chest X ray helps a doctor see if your heart is healthy.

Doing a physical exam. During the exam, the doctor might draw blood or ask for a urine sample. Urine is the body's liquid waste. Blood and urine are tested to rule out any disorders for which HBP may be a symptom. Your blood pressure, pulse, height, weight, and reflexes probably will be recorded. The doctor may feel your stomach and back to see if any organs feel larger than normal.

Looking at the blood vessels in your eyes with a small scope. High blood pressure can damage the blood vessels in your eyes. The doctor is looking for signs of damage such as thickening, narrowing, or bleeding in your eye blood vessels.

Taking an X ray of your chest. Your doctor may order a chest X ray to see if your heart is enlarged, or larger than normal.

Reading the electrical impulses of your heart with an electrocardiograph. This test also can show if your heart is enlarged. Little round sensors are placed on the skin around your chest. Wires run from the sensors to a machine that traces lines on a strip of paper. The lines also can show if blocked arteries have damaged the heart.

You can act to make sure your blood pressure readings are accurate and consistent.

• Wear short or loose sleeves that you can roll above your elbow to make room for the blood pressure cuff.

• Don't eat, smoke, exercise, or drink coffee or tea at least half an hour before your blood pressure is measured.

• Use the same arm each time your pressure is checked.

• Sit calmly and don't cross your legs before your blood pressure reading.

Your doctor will take all of the information from these tests and decide if you have high blood pressure. If you do, your health care professional will help you develop a treatment plan to lower your blood pressure.

"Isn't there some kind of pill you can give me to fix my blood pressure?" Gabe asked his doctor. Dr. Martin said that first she wanted Gabe to try changing his diet and exercising more. She told Gabe his HBP was mild. The pills would come later if Gabe couldn't lower his blood pressure with some changes in how he lived. Gabe felt that it would be too hard to eat differently and exercise more. Dr. Martin explained that learning to do those things would prevent lots of health problems later. Gabe thought some more and decided to work with Dr. Martin. He wasn't sure he wanted to take the medication anyway. Even headache medicine made him feel dizzy.

Gabe, Age 13

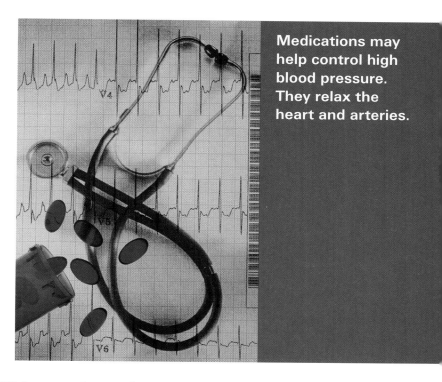

Medications may help control high blood pressure. They relax the heart and arteries.

No cure exists for HBP, but you almost always can control it. For people with mild to moderate HBP, treatment includes changing what you eat and getting regular exercise. Chapter 5 discusses more of these and other lifestyle changes. Medication may be used if the blood pressure doesn't respond to healthier living.

People with severe to very severe HBP usually start lifestyle treatment and medication right away to control their blood pressure. More than three-fourths of people with HBP control it using medication with a diet and exercise plan. When medicines are prescribed, only one or a combination may be used.

Your doctor may try different medicines before finding the right combination. Medicines work in different ways to treat HBP. Your doctor might ask you to take diuretics, beta-blockers, calcium-channel blockers, or vasodilators. These are just a few of the names, but the drugs all do two important things. They relax the arteries and keep the heart from pumping too hard.

Work with your doctor to treat your high blood pressure. Follow instructions for taking any medication. Keep track of your blood pressure readings on a chart so you can see changes for yourself. On a sheet of paper, just list the date of the reading and what the reading was. For example, "June 27: 140 over 90. June 30: 132 over 84." It's important not to miss any medical appointments.

You may want to learn to take your own measurements so you can chart more readings. You can do this at your local pharmacy or grocery store. Some people buy portable equipment to measure their blood pressure at home. Your parents' medical insurance may or may not cover the cost of home equipment.

It's important to remember that controlling your HBP doesn't mean fixing it. Your grandfather might wear hearing aids. When he does, he can hear things better and be a part of things. He still has a hearing problem, though. If he doesn't wear his hearing aids, he can't hear everything. Controlling your HBP is not much different from your grandfather controlling his hearing. You still have the condition, but by managing it, you can lead a normal, active life.

"I take my medicine in the morning with a glass of water after I brush my teeth. It's part of my morning routine."—Kylie, age 15

"I wash down my vitamins and medication with a glass of milk at dinner."—Cort, age 14

"I taped a note to my mirror that says, 'Take your meds, Miguel!'"—Miguel, age 18

Points to Consider

What's one way you can make your lifestyle healthier? For example, could you walk up steps instead of taking an elevator?

Why do you think people sometimes have a hard time managing their high blood pressure?

Imagine you needed to do three things when you were 13 to get your driver's license at 16. Would you do them? Living a healthier lifestyle now will help you to prevent HBP and other diseases later. Do you think this is the same as working toward something you really want, such as your license? Explain.

Chapter Overview

You can do three key things to prevent or manage your high blood pressure. These are to control your weight, eat a balanced low-fat, low-cholesterol diet, and exercise regularly.

More and more teens are overweight. As a result, more teens have high blood pressure than ever before.

It's important to reduce the amount of salt you eat, take a multivitamin, and learn to relax. Visit your doctor regularly.

Chapter 5

Lifestyle Changes:
Taming the Blood Pressure Beast

Studies show that even small lifestyle changes in the elderly can help them bring down their HBP. When you're taking medicine for HBP, lifestyle changes may be even more effective. This should hold true for anyone, young or old. There are three key things you can do on your own to reduce your risk of getting HBP. They are the same three things you would do to control your HBP if you already had it.

Three Strikes and You're Out of the HBP Ballpark

Recent research found that probably the three most important things you can do to prevent and manage high blood pressure are:

Lose Those Extra Pounds If You're Carrying Them Around

Work with your doctor to agree on an ideal weight for you. The latest research shows that permanent, moderate weight loss can prevent HBP. Overweight teens and adults greatly increase their risk of getting HBP and serious diseases.

People who are overweight or obese often have high cholesterol, too. American diets, and to a lesser extent Canadian diets, are loaded with fat, cholesterol, and saturated fat. Saturated fat comes from animals and animal products such as butter. That's one reason more teens and adults are overweight today than ever before.

Eat a Balanced, Low-Saturated-Fat, Low-Cholesterol Diet

Eating to tame your blood pressure beast means picking foods that are low in saturated fat and cholesterol. Saturated fat is loaded with cholesterol. Controlling fat in your diet usually makes losing weight easier, and it lowers your cholesterol levels.

Broiling, baking, or steaming your food is better for your heart than frying the food.

The U.S. Food Guide Pyramid and Canadian Food Guide to Healthy Eating are good places to start. They show the right foods to eat to balance your diet. You can find copies of the pyramid and rainbow on many cereal boxes or posters in your school. You might see them in pamphlets available from your health care provider. You can read more about the Food Guide Pyramid and a balanced diet. Books listed in the For More Information section at the back of this book can help you. Here are some tips to reduce fat and cholesterol in your diet:

Broil and bake, don't fry.

Avoid creamy salad dressings on your salads. Order the dressing on the side and dip your fork in it to get the flavor of the dressing in every bite.

Eat part-skim and nonfat cheeses. Use sharp, flavorful cheeses so you eat less.

Don't drown your meal in sauces and gravy. Skip them altogether or only dress your food with fatty sauces as an occasional treat.

You're likely to continue exercising if you pick something you enjoy doing.

Get and Stay Active

Regular exercise helps you feel and look better. If you don't have physical education at school or don't play a sport, you can still get active. Ride a bike, swim, run, or jog. Walk instead of taking the bus. Make it your mission to move.

People who exercise are more likely to maintain a healthy weight. Exercise lowers blood cholesterol and blood pressure. Regular physical activity also gives you more energy, lowers stress, and helps you sleep better. Those benefits begin on day one.

Woody used to hate to exercise. He just couldn't get into running or jogging. Then he discovered in-line skating. He skates everywhere now.

Woody, Age 16

Like Woody, be sure to pick activities you enjoy. If you don't like the activity, you probably won't do it. And when we say regular exercise, we're not talking about shooting hoops once a month. We're talking about an activity you can do for half an hour three or more times a week. Work up a sweat.

Smoking is one of the worst things you can do to your cardiovascular system.

Plan long-term and short-term goals. Talk with your doctor about your exercise plans if you haven't exercised much before.

Now What?

Okay, you've tackled the big three. You're losing weight, eating better, and exercising more. Now what do you do? Studies show a few more cards are still in your winning hand.

Don't Start Smoking, or If You Already Smoke, Quit

Smoking doesn't cause high blood pressure. But it is one of the most dangerous things you can do to your cardiovascular system. It cuts your life short, ages your skin, and weakens your lungs and heart. Not only that, but you may stink and can get yellow fingernails.

It's hard to quit smoking, so be smart and don't start. If you do smoke, set a target date now to quit smoking. Mark your calendar. Tell your family and friends you're quitting. Ask a friend or family member to quit with you.

Quitting won't be easy. You may have withdrawal symptoms from the cigarettes' nicotine, which is a drug. Your mouth might feel dry, you may feel hungry, and you probably will be a grouch. Other symptoms may include coughing, dizziness, or headaches. It will take several days to several weeks for your body to stop craving nicotine. It will take your mind much longer.

The first three months after quitting, you might automatically reach for a cigarette as a way to relax. Try to find other ways to relax. Take a bath. Go for a walk. Call a friend. You may slip up and smoke a cigarette after quitting. Even if you slip, don't give up. Quit again. And again. And again if you have to. Many successful former smokers quit for good only after several tries.

Park Your Salt Cravings
Most people eat way too much salt. It causes the body to hold on to water. Extra water gets into the blood, too, which means there's more fluid in your blood vessels. The extra fluid creates higher blood pressure.

"My mom, grandfather, and uncle all have high blood pressure. I don't have it—yet. My doc says I can do some things to feel better, look great, and lower my chances of high blood pressure. In my wallet next to the photos of my family, I keep a list of things the doctor said I can do. I look at it sometimes to remind me to be careful and take care of myself."
—Nueva, age 16

Limiting the amount of salt you eat each day can moderately affect your HBP risk. But don't just hide the salt shaker. Most of the salt you eat comes from processed and packaged foods. In fact, more than 80 percent does. Even some medications have salt in them.

Eating more fruits and vegetables instead of junk food will help get rid of some of the salt in your diet. Read food labels. Even a fast-food milkshake is loaded with salt. So ask fast-food cashiers how much salt is in their food.

Take Nutrient "Insurance"

This isn't the kind of insurance your mother has on her car. No, we're talking about vitamin supplements. If you're not sure you're getting enough nutrients such as potassium, calcium, or magnesium, take a multivitamin.

The latest research shows a strong link between potassium and reducing the risk of getting HBP. People even may lower their HBP when they get enough potassium in their diet. Making sure you get enough calcium and magnesium in your diet also may lower blood pressure.

Did You Know?

When someone says you've inherited high blood pressure from your family, you've inherited the risk, not the condition. You still may not get HBP. You can reduce your risk, even with a family history of HBP. Do this by eating right, exercising, not smoking, and keeping a normal weight. Be sure to take your medication if your doctor has prescribed some.

Learn to Manage Your Stress

Controlling how you react to stress helps in two ways. It improves your health. And it keeps you from falling back on bad habits such as smoking and eating too much. Battling stressful situations may be good for you once in a while. It actually can help energize your mind and body. Your body produces the stress-fighting substance epinephrine, or adrenaline, when you face stress triggers. Anything that makes you worried or anxious is a stress trigger. However, long-term or chronic stress can wear you down, make you sick, and raise your blood pressure.

Arliss feels like she's going to explode. Home, school, work, and sports are pulling her in a thousand different directions. She looks and feels tired all the time. She isn't happy and hardly ever smiles. This morning she yelled at her little brother for spilling some of her favorite perfume. "What's wrong with me?" Arliss says to the mirror as she puts makeup over the dark circles under her eyes.

Arliss, Age 17

Feeling stressed all the time like Arliss isn't good for your body and mind. You can feel tired and miserable. How much you suffer from stress depends on your reaction to stress triggers. The next page shows a few stress-battling pointers.

Advice
From Teens

No surprises! Plan your day when you can.

Set realistic personal and school goals.

Adapt to stressful situations instead of fighting them. Does your mom keep busting you for breaking curfew? Maybe she'll agree to later curfews if you let her know where you are more often. You'll both feel better if you can agree on something.

Exercise to release epinephrine.

Make time each day to do something for you. If you love taking naps, try to squeeze a short one in now and then.

Write down your feelings in a journal. Just getting the words out may help you feel better.

Before getting out of bed in the morning, place your hand on the skin below your stomach and breathe deeply. Feel your hand rising and falling with each breath. This sort of deep breathing can help you relax before you start your day.

The phone is helpful in reducing high blood pressure. You can use it to call for a medical appointment.

See Your Doctor

The teen years can be difficult. Teens may wrestle with alcohol and other drug abuse, pregnancy, smoking, depression, or killing themselves. Many teens develop unhealthy lifestyle habits such as smoking and drinking. Most of these habits continue into adulthood. It's important to see a health care professional as regularly as possible as a teen. This is especially true if you don't play sports that require a physical exam.

Make an appointment at least every two years to get an exam. Get your cholesterol and blood pressure checked. Try to check your blood pressure even more frequently at pharmacies or grocery stores. Many of these stores have a blood pressure machine you can use. Community organizations often offer free blood pressure screening. If you don't have medical insurance to cover a visit, try to save the money you need. Check the *Community* listing in your telephone book for free and reduced-fee medical clinics.

Olive oil is believed to prevent heart disease. A 12-month Italian study had people replace saturated fats in their diet with olive oil. The findings showed that the people lowered their blood pressure. Doctors are not sure how the olive oil does this. More research needs to be done to unravel that mystery.

Into the Future

Don't Drink Alcohol

Alcohol has a lot of calories, and drinking can cause people to gain weight. Weight gain, as we've seen, makes it difficult to control high blood pressure. And don't forget: Drinking is illegal for teens.

Points to Consider

Name three high-salt foods you eat each week that you could cut down on.

Your days are jammed, but can you think of one way that you could get more active? For example, could you walk or bike to your part-time job?

Do you smoke? Why or why not? What might you tell a friend to help him or her stop smoking?

Chapter Overview

High blood pressure is nothing to be afraid of. It can be prevented and treated.

Taking care of yourself emotionally and physically will help you prevent or control HBP.

Many places exist for HBP information and help. These include friends, family, and medical professionals. Many organizations are good sources, too.

Teens can begin HBP prevention habits now. They also can support family and friends who have high blood pressure.

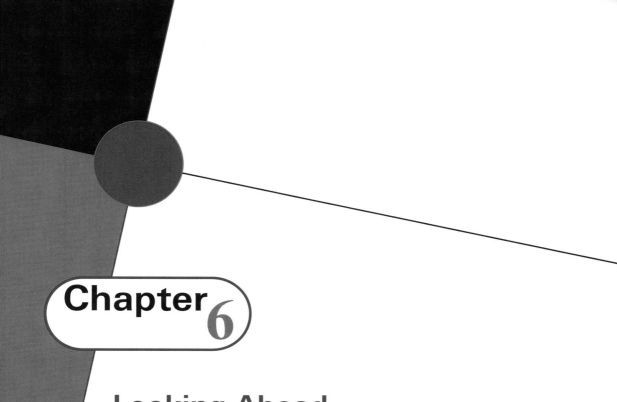

Chapter 6

Looking Ahead

Don't let high blood pressure frighten you. It can be prevented and treated. New research helps doctors better understand how to battle HBP. One study has shown that if you don't take your HBP medicine as prescribed, you can increase your stroke risk.

Another study recently showed that controlling HBP now can help reduce the effects of hardening of the arteries later. Your natural mental decline with aging may lessen if you control HBP. Researchers also have identified a "salt gene" that may predict how well you might respond to lifestyle changes to fight HBP.

Did You Know?

A recent study found that women with HBP are more likely to break their bones than women without HBP.

With these new techniques, doctors will be able to better plan your treatment now. A simple blood test might tell your doctor if you're likely to need medication with your lifestyle changes. Medication could be prescribed right away instead of waiting to see what effect just lifestyle changes have on you.

Take Care of You

No matter what time it is, Shawn ends every day with a long, hot shower and a glass of warm milk before bed. It helps her unwind. Once in a while, she can't do these things. Then she always wakes up the next morning feeling less rested.

Shawn, Age 17

Your doctor can work with you to prevent or manage high blood pressure. You can lead a normal lifestyle with HBP. The trick is to control it before it leads to serious complications such as heart disease and stroke. Try to eat right and be active. Don't smoke. Help your doctor develop a plan to improve your overall health. Find time to do things that make you feel happy. Learn to relax.

You may understand your feelings better if you write about them.

Let your friends and family know you have HBP. Tell them that you want to improve your lifestyle to manage it in the future. With or without HBP, you can be a healthy, active teen.

Dealing With Your Feelings About HBP

You might have questions or be confused about your feelings. One way to deal with your questions and feelings about HBP is to write them down in a journal or notebook. Writing about your feelings can make you feel more in control of your life. Journaling can help you come up with creative ways to handle healthy lifestyle challenges. At the least, you may feel better after writing some of your thoughts on paper.

After you've written down some of your questions and thoughts, talk to a doctor. He or she is the best place to start for information about HBP. He or she can point you in the right direction for more information, too.

Your school nurse or local clinic can provide information, too. Your health care provider can give you the names of local support groups, which share information with their members. Some groups may be listed in your telephone book.

The rate of deaths that strokes cause has dropped dramatically. One report showed that from **1971** to **1994**, the rate dropped **70** percent for some groups of people.

Whether you have high blood pressure or not, there are organizations and government agencies with excellent information. The American Heart Association, the American Stroke Association, and the Canadian Heart and Stroke Foundation provide information in brochures and on their Internet sites. Government agencies can provide quality information about heart disease and its prevention. The section of Useful Addresses and Internet Sites on page 62 shows you how to reach these resources.

When You Don't Have HBP

You might not have HBP. You may never get it. But don't wait for it to sneak up on you. Do whatever it takes to reduce your risk of HBP. Chapter 5 talked about the most important things you can do to prevent HBP. Don't keep this information to yourself. Spread the word. Talk with your friends and family about living a healthy lifestyle. Begin a "Commit to Be Fit" group at school. The group can eat healthy meals and snacks together. You all can exercise together.

Friends and family can help support each other in fighting high blood pressure.

Support friends and family who have HBP. Ask them how you can help. Offer to exercise with them, cook them low-fat meals, hide their cigarettes, or just listen to their feelings. If you've already turned your bad habits into good ones, help a friend change his or her lifestyle. Fix healthy snacks for both of you to munch at school.

Just Do It

"My dad can barely see because of high blood pressure. It really messed up his eyes. I don't want to be like that. I'm going to do what it takes to make sure I don't get HBP. Or that I take control if I do get it someday."

Michael, Age 14

Michael has the right attitude, but he'll meet a lot of obstacles on the way to his goal. Many of those obstacles come from within. You know you need to reduce your risk of HBP, but you just don't know how to start. You might feel like you'll never be able to make all the changes.

Into the Future

Microchips are being developed that can spot tiny genetic differences in humans. These little differences are called "snips." Snips often mean nothing. Sometimes, though, having a snip can mean you're more likely to get a disease. Someday, babies might be tested at birth, and their genetic information will be put on a chip. When the chip's information is read in a special instrument, it may help doctors predict, treat, and prevent diseases.

The first step is commitment. Write down what you need to do to lead a healthier life. If you have a lot of risk factors to deal with, pick an easy one to change first. When you've done that, move to the next one. For example if you need to exercise more and lose weight, begin with exercise. When you settle into a regular routine, begin to add some healthy habits to your eating routine. Cut down on fat, eat less salt, and watch your weight.

Living in a way that reduces the risk of high blood pressure is a win-win situation. You're taking steps to lower your risk of developing HBP and cardiovascular diseases. At the same time, you're getting fit and becoming healthier. You'll look your best and feel great. What's not to like about that?

Everyone wins by reducing high blood pressure.

Points to Consider

What are three things you could do to offer emotional support to a family member with HBP?

Name some places you could go to get HBP information.

How do you think keeping track of your goals to manage HBP can help you?

Glossary

artery (AR-tuh-ree)—flexible tube of tissue in the body that carries blood

atherosclerosis (ATH-uh-roh-skluh-roh-suhss)—a condition in which the arteries become scarred, less flexible, thicker, and hardened

cardiovascular system (car-dee-oh-VASS-kyuh-lur SISS-tuhm)—the parts of the body that work together to move blood, oxygen, and carbon dioxide; the heart, lungs, and blood vessels make up the body's cardiovascular system.

cholesterol (kuh-LESS-tuh-rol)—a fat-like nutrient from animals that people need to digest food and make certain vitamins; too much cholesterol in the body can mean a higher risk for heart disease.

circulation (sur-kyuh-LAY-shuhn)—the movement of blood around your body

diastolic pressure (dye-uh-STOL-ik PRESH-ur)—the pressure in the arteries when the heart relaxes and fills with blood

hypertension (hye-pur-TEN-shuhn)—high blood pressure

nutrient (NOO-tree-uhnt)—something in food that is needed for people to grow, repair the body, and stay healthy

obese (oh-BEESS)—very overweight

sodium (SOH-dee-uhm)—a part of salt; many people use the words *salt* and *sodium* to mean the same thing.

sphygmomanometer (sfig-moh-muh-NOM-uh-tur)—a cuff that wraps around the arm, used for measuring blood pressure

stethoscope (STETH-uh-skope)—device used to listen to the heart and lungs

symptom (SIMP-tuhm)—something that shows that a person has an illness, condition, or disease

systolic pressure (siss-STOL-ik PRESH-ur)—pressure in the arteries when the heart pumps blood

For More Information

Gregson, Susan R. *Heart Disease.* Mankato, MN: Capstone, 2001.

Jenkins, Mark. *High Blood Pressure: Practical, Medical and Spiritual Guidelines for Daily Living With Hypertension.* Minneapolis: Hazelden Pocket Health Guides, 1999.

Perry, Angela. *The AMA Essential Guide to Hypertension.* New York: Pocket Books, 1998.

Turck, Mary. *Healthy Eating for Weight Management.* Mankato, MN: Capstone, 2001.

 At publication, all resources listed here were accurate and appropriate to the topics covered in this book. Addresses and phone numbers may change. When visiting Internet sites and links, use good judgment. Remember, never give personal information over the Internet.

Useful Addresses and Internet Sites

American Heart Association (AHA)
American Stroke Association
(division of AHA)
National Center
7272 Greenville Avenue
Dallas, TX 75231
www.americanheart.org
www.americanstroke.org
1-800-AHA-USA1 (1-800-242-8721)

Heart and Stroke Foundation of Canada
222 Queen Street
Suite 1402
Ottawa, ON K1P 5V9
CANADA
www.hsf.ca

National Heart, Lung, and Blood Institute
(NHLBI)
National Institutes of Health
NHLBI Information Center
PO Box 30105
Bethesda, MD 20824-0105
www.nhlbi.nih.gov
1-800-575-WELL (1-800-575-9355)

American Dietetic Association (ADA)
www.eatright.org
Great tips for healthy and low-salt eating

Health Canada
www.hc-sc.gc.ca
A–Z health topic index and information

The Hypertension Network
www.bloodpressure.com
Information on high blood pressure causes
and treatment

Index

age, 11, 24
alcohol, 50, 51
American Heart Association, 8, 56
anger, 5
anxiety, 33, 48
arteries, 6–8, 15–17, 19, 20, 32, 37, 53
atherosclerosis, 6

blood pressure, measuring, 8, 18,
    31–32, 33, 34, 36, 38, 50
blood vessels, 6–7, 15–17, 35, 46
brain, 6, 7, 16

Canadian Food Guide to Healthy
    Eating, 43
carbon dioxide, 17
cardiovascular system, 15, 16, 45
cholesterol, 26, 42, 43, 44, 50
circulation, 15–21
circulatory system, 17
coronary heart disease, 19

death, 7, 20, 56
depression, 10, 50
diabetes, 25
diastolic pressure, 8, 32
diet, 9, 12, 18, 26–27, 36–37, 42–43,
    46, 47, 48, 54, 56–58. *See also*
    cholesterol; fat in diet; salt
doctors, 7, 23, 24, 34–38, 42, 50, 51,
    54, 58

electrocardiograph, 35
essential hypertension, 23
excitement, 5
exercise, 9, 12, 19, 26, 36–37, 44–45,
    49, 54, 56–58
eyes, 6, 20, 21, 35, 57

family history, 9, 24, 25, 34, 47, 48
fat in diet, 12, 26, 27, 42–43, 57, 58
fear, 5
Food Guide Pyramid, 43

gender, 24
government agencies, 56

habits, 11, 25–27, 48, 50, 57
Hales, Stephen, 18
Harvey, William, 19
heart, 6, 8, 15, 16–17, 19, 20, 26, 31,
    32, 35, 37, 43, 45, 54
high blood pressure
    causes and risks of, 23–29
    charting, 38
    controlling and preventing, 11, 12,
        13, 38, 41, 42–51, 54, 56
    diagnosing, 31–35
    learning about, 11, 34
    measuring, 8, 18, 31–32, 34, 36,
        38, 50
    ranges for, 8, 33
    treating, 36–39
    what is it?, 5–13
    who gets it?, 9

Index continued

journals, 38, 49, 55

kidneys, 6, 20, 23, 24

lifestyle changes, 11, 18, 19, 25,
    36–37, 41–51, 53–55, 57
low blood pressure, 8, 10

medications, 25, 36–39, 41, 48, 49,
    53, 54
myths, 9

nervousness, 33
nutrients, 6, 15, 47

organizations, 56
oxygen, 6, 7, 15, 17, 20

pain, 31, 33
pregnancy, 24, 50
prevention, 11, 12, 13, 25, 26, 38, 41,
    42–51, 54, 56, 58
pulmonary circuit, 16

race, 9, 25, 56
relaxation, 26, 46, 49, 54
risk quiz, 28–29
risks, 23–29, 41, 58

salt, 9, 12, 19, 24–27, 46–47, 53, 58
secondary hypertension, 23
shock, 10
smoking, 9, 12, 26, 45–46, 48, 50,
    54, 57
sodium. *See* salt
sphygmomanometer, 32
stress, 5, 26, 33, 44
    managing, 48–49
strokes, 7, 19, 26, 29, 31, 53, 54, 56
    signs of, 7, 20
suicide, 50
support, 55, 57
swelling, 19
systemic circuit, 16
systolic pressure, 8, 32

tiredness, 10, 19, 48
treatment, 36–39

veins, 15–17
vitamin supplements, 47

weakness, 10, 19
weight, 9, 11, 24, 25, 42, 44, 48, 51,
    58

X rays, 35